What is This?

Jane Wood

OXFORD

Can you see what this is?
Is it a dog or a cat?

Yes! It is a dog.

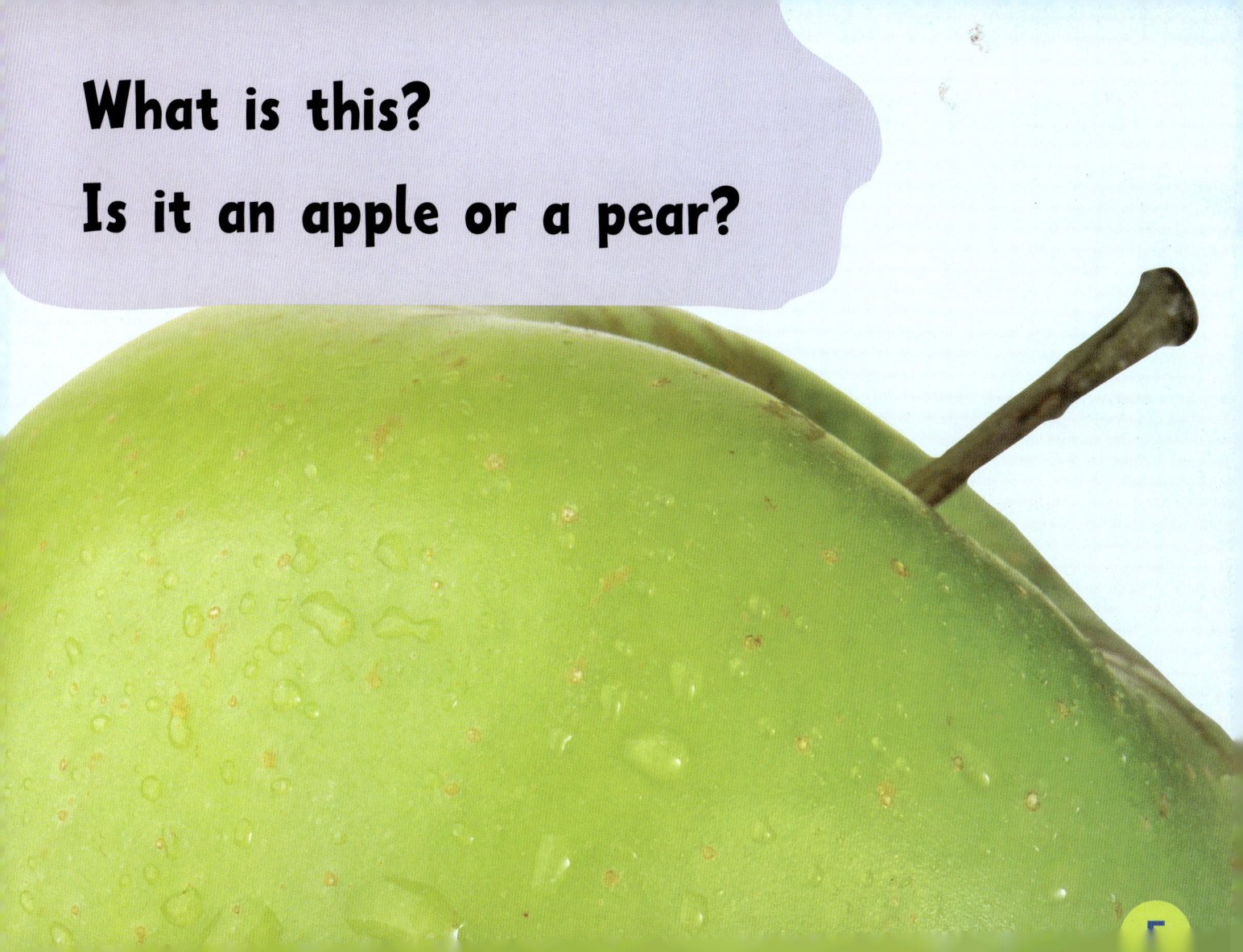

What is this?
Is it an apple or a pear?

It is an apple.

Can you see what this is?

It is a bike.

Can you see what this is?

It is a toothbrush.

What is this?

11

It is a shoe.

What are these?

These are pencils.

Is this a bird or is it a butterfly?

It is a butterfly!